What's the elf

The elf on a shelf tradition linked to Christmas celebrations is a delightful and imaginative practice that seeks to enhance the excitement of Christmas for kids. As per this tradition, an elf, usually depicted as Santa Claus's helper, comes to houses on December 1st. Each night, as the family sleeps, the elf sets up a small prank or arranges a funny scenario by causing mischief. These scenarios are typically harmless and meant to inspire awe and happiness in children.

Every morning, when they wake up, the kids find the elf's latest prank with surprise and joy. This daily routine is a special time that brings excitement and playfulness to the days leading up to Christmas. On December 25, Christmas Day, the elf says goodbye to join Santa Claus. Before departing, the elf usually leaves a small note for the child, making his farewell feel personal and heartfelt.

This book targets parents who want to continue this lovely tradition. It provides many creative ideas for setting up the elf each night, suggesting pranks and unique scenes that will surprise kids and enhance family Christmas memories. Whether it's through funny scenes, playful notes, or heartwarming moments, the mischievous elf turns into a special visitor who brings joy and enchantment into houses throughout the festive period.

Here's a sample of a letter that Elfie can write on the day it arrives:

Dear (Child's Name), Hey there! I'm Elfie, and I come from a faraway, snowy place where I help Santa Claus. You know what ? Santa Claus let me have a little break, and I decided to spend it here, with you !

I'm really looking forward to sharing these special Advent moments. I'm going to chill out and have a blast, but sometimes I can be a bit clumsy, and surprises might pop up. I can assure you that everything will be filled with happiness and laughter.

Every morning, you can discover what I did overnight. Maybe you'll come across hints of my small nighttime escapades. I wish this brings a smile to your face and brings extra happiness to your day as you count down to Christmas.

I'll behave... well, I'll try! But after all, I'm a leprechaun, and leprechauns like to have fun. So who knows what could happen?

On Christmas morning, I'll head back to the North Pole. But for now, get ready for surprises and plenty of laughter. I can't wait to enjoy this wonderful time of year with you.

With all my love and a touch of playfulness, Elfie.

DEAR PARENTS

On the next pages, you'll discover many fun ideas using everyday items to keep your kids entertained in the morning. And, let's admit it, parents will have fun too!

1 When the elf comes, flip various containers on the living room floor. Bowls, pots, pans, or salad bowls, and leave a note from the elf saying he's hidden! Let's find it !

2 Wrap toilet paper all over the house. You can drape it over furniture, suspend it from the ceiling, or even rip it into small bits to create a trail for the elf.

Fill the sink with bubbles or **3**
soapy suds, with the elf in the
center, as if having a foam
party.

Imagine a holiday setting **4**
with the elf relaxing on a
small beach towel, wearing
paper sunglasses and
sunscreen.

5 Arrange a scenario where the elf teaches toys how to paint using tiny canvases and brushes.

6 Add small red paper noses or draw clown noses on family photos using an erasable marker, with the elf holding a pencil or piece of paper.

Make a big paper airplane and **7**
put the elf inside, like he's
flying. You could hang the
airplane from the ceiling for a
cooler look.

Stuff a long-sleeved shirt and
pants with cushions or **8**
newspaper and have the elf's
head peeking out, as if he were
wearing them.

9 Hide the elf in the refrigerator with a note mentioning how he longed for the chill of the North Pole!

10 Sprinkle flour on the kitchen table. Place the elf on the flour and have him move his arms and legs to create a mark in the flour like a snow angel!

Move the furniture in a room. **11**
For instance, adjust the position
of the kitchen table or place
the chairs around it and let the
elf sit on one.

Conceal the elf inside an **12**
empty bottle with a small
note saying "oops...I was
thirsty"

13 Place the elf inside an empty tissue box, with tissues acting as a pillow and blanket, as if he is sleeping soundly.

14 Put the elf in front of the TV with the remote in hand, and have some candy, popcorn, or treats around, like he's watching a movie.

Construct a pyramid or another **15**
building using toilet paper rolls,
   and then hide the elf inside.

Hang a pair of underwear on   **16**
   the wall with the elf inside,
   as if he were wearing them.

17 Arrange shoes in a row, like a train, with the elf as the "conductor" at the front.

18 Draw a tic-tac-toe game on the mirror using an erasable marker, with the elf holding the marker, all set to play.

Arrange a race with small cars, **19** with the elf as the driver of one car, all set up on a makeshift track.

Arrange the elf capturing a **20** group photo of stuffed animals in front of the Christmas tree using a small camera or phone.

21 Put many socks in a big pot with water, like the elf made sock "soup".

22 Change the phone's wallpaper to a funny picture or photo of the leprechaun, and place the phone next to it.

Use a marker to draw faces or **23**
patterns on the eggs in the
fridge, with the elf next to
them.

Draw mustaches on the family
photos using an erasable marker,**24**
with the elf holding the marker.
You can also cut whiskers out of
the paper.

25 Place tape over your child's bedroom door to make it tricky for them to leave without taking it off. Hand the tape roll to the elf.

26 Display the elf preparing breakfast, with kitchen tools and ingredients all around.

Watch the elf climb a shelf or piece of furniture, using a rope to reach a box of cakes, for instance.

Stack three toilet paper rolls on top of each other. Draw a snowman's face on the top roll and hide the elf inside. **28**

29 Fill the sink with a bit of water, then put the elf in and add some bath toys or a small buoy.

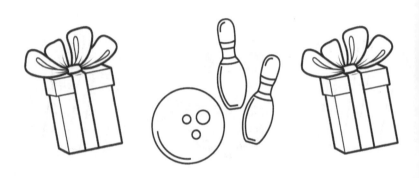

30 Prepare a game of bowling with a ball and water bottles as pins, and have the elf all set to throw the ball.

Create a tiny swing with an **31** empty toilet paper roll and some string. Attach the string to a door jamb and place the elf on the roll.

Put the elf next to the sink **32** filled with water, pretending to fish with a small fishing rod.

33 Set up a little cushion slide for the elf and their soft toy friends to sled down.

34 Wake your child up gently with music by placing the elf on the music source, as if he's the one who turned it on. Pick some Christmas carols!

Place a tray of water in the **35** freezer and dip the elf in it. Make sure to stretch out your arms and legs. The next morning, you'll find him frozen in a block of ice!

Construct a cabin using **36** books and hide the elf inside, reading a book with a flashlight!

37 Put the elf in a tiny boat or bowl with sticks for paddles in the sink, like he's going on an adventure.

38 Open the drawers of a dresser in your child's room and place all the mixed clothes on the floor with the elf perched at the very top of the pile.

Wrap the elf in aluminum foil, **39** place a glass securely on his head taped to the body, and leave a note saying he is returning from space.

Place the elf in a seated position **40** and surround him with tiny clumps of soil. Grab a little present for your child, and attach a message stating: "I discovered this hidden gem in the garden for you."

41 Create a large cape for the elf using toilet paper. Hang it from the ceiling for a more impressive look.

42 Arrange the elf practicing yoga, with little dolls or stuffed animals copying the poses around.

Fasten the elf to some balloons, **43**
letting him float in the air like
he's off on an aerial journey.

Make a cotton ball battle **44**
scene with the elf and other
toys.

45 Give the elf a marker and scatter multiple drawings around him as if he had been drawing all night.

46 Arrange the elf with an open book, surrounded by figurines or dolls, as if he were reading them a story.

Put the elf in a martial arts **47** stance, with small obstacles or bricks around, like he's training to break them.

Display the elf "tattooing" **48** cute designs using washable markers on dolls or applying temporary tattoos.

49 Place bandages on the leprechaun's head and sit him next to a banana peel as though he slipped on it.

50 Place branches, leaves, and stones around the elf with a note saying: "I went for a hike last night!"

Imagine the elf writing a postcard to **51**
Santa Claus. Let's read the postcard
together where he talks about his stay
and the children. He praises the
children and mentions that he
doesn't do anything silly!

Create a leprechaun **52**
parachute using a paper bag
and string. Hang it up high
as if it got stuck while
jumping.

53 Make a hammock for the mischievous elf using a surgical mask.

54 Imagine a scenario where the elf is playing cards or a board game with figurines or stuffed animals. Perhaps he's being sneaky by hiding cards behind his back!

Place an egg in a bowl near the **55** elf. Remember to leave a small container labeled "magic cocoa". Include a note requesting the child to sprinkle the magic cocoa on the egg...

The next day, swap the egg **56** for a chocolate egg!

57 Spread sand or flour and hide pretend bones in it. Give the elf a paintbrush as if they were on an archaeological adventure.

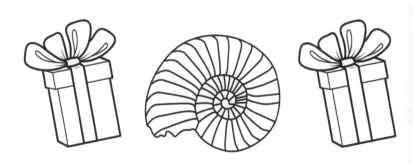

58 Cut out the page opposite and make a hole at the top to fit the elf's head through.

Create a small bow for the elf **59**
using a piece of wood and some
string. Make arrows out of
toothpicks and shoot them into
a target such as an apple or
cereal box.

Make a tiny pétanque set **60**
using little marbles and a
jack. The elf plays with other
figurines or stuffed animals.

61 Arrange the elf with tiny bottles and flowers, like he's making a perfume.

62 Set up the elf crafting tiny masks using colored paper and rubber bands. You can even use a picture of your child to create a mask!

Leave a message from the elf that **63**
reads: "I played a prank on your
dad, check out his toes!" You should
have already painted your nails or
colored your feet with a marker.

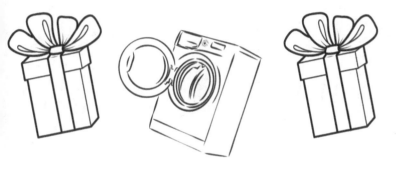

Put the elf in the washing **64**
machine drum with a note
that says: "Ready for the
ride!"

65 Cut out the next page to create the outline of Santa Claus. Place the elf near a desk lamp, and illuminate the paper outline to project Santa's shadow on the wall.

66 Set up a tight rope between two spots and have the elf balance on it.

Sketch a soccer field on a piece **67** of paper and share a game plan. Place the elf as if they are teaching the plan to other toys or plushies.

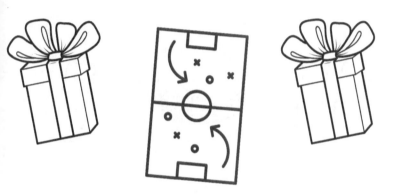

Put the elf together with puzzle pieces, like solving a puzzle. You **68** can draw on the back of the puzzle. Your little one can put the puzzle together to reveal the elf's drawing.

69 Make some pancakes and wrap the elf in one of them, then place it on top of the stack of pancakes. Create a hole at eye level to peek at the elf.

70 Remove a few garlands from the tree and place them around the elf as if he playfully took them off.

Wrap a piece of furniture with **71** wrapping paper and place the elf on it. You can also do this with the toilet!

Put glasses on the elf's nose **72** while he works on crosswords or sudoku.

73 Remove the eyes from the page and stick them on objects like cans, a toy box, or a backpack. Put the sheet next to the elf with scissors.

74 Construct a staircase using books and position a diving board at the top. Below the diving board, put a soup plate filled with water. An elf stands on the diving board, cheered on by the stuffed animals near the plate.

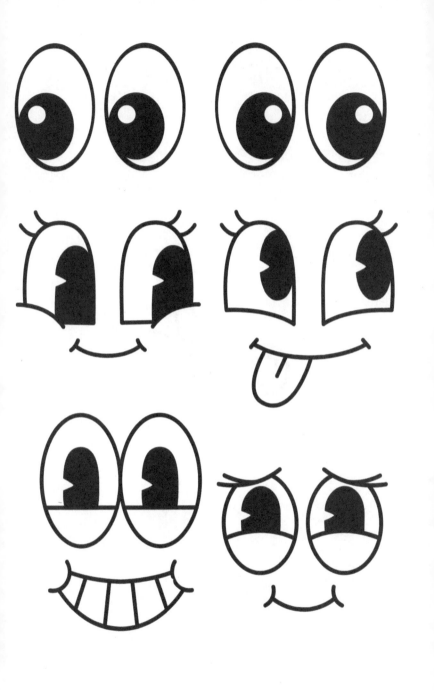

75 Unwind a ball of yarn all over the house, beginning in the kids' room and threading it through unexpected spots. Place the elf at the end of the yarn.

76 Snap a picture of the elf with your little one while they are sleeping. Place the elf close to the phone with the screen lit up.

Place the elf next to a makeup set. **77**
Put on extremely bold makeup as if
the elf did your makeup while you
were sleeping. Pretend you have no
idea!

Save empty toilet paper rolls **78**
for a few weeks and create a
genuine elf castle using a's
glue gun.

79 Wrap the Christmas tree with toilet paper and place the elf at the base of the tree.

80 Put the elf in the driver's seat of your car or on your child's car seat. You'll only discover it when you head to school!

Place the elf, various figurines, **81**
and stuffed animals inside a
sock, making it look like a
sleeping bag. Position them in a
circle resembling a campfire.

Put some hooks on the tree **82**
and hang the elf on one of
them.

83 Wrap the Christmas tree with toilet paper and place the elf at the base of the tree.

84 Plant the elf in a pot using a small spoon as a shovel. Place some soil beside the pot and a small treat in the hole.

Put the elf beside a slice of **85**
chocolate toast, with chocolate
on his mouth, like he had eaten
it overnight.

Attach the elf to a window **86**
outside the house with a
message that reads: "I left
without taking the keys,
help!"

87 Fold multiple sheets of toilet paper without separating them and cut into pieces. Unfold the sheets to create a lace effect. Let the roll hang in this way.

88 If it snows at your house, put the elf outside while it's snowing, sitting, and visible from indoors so that in the morning, only part of its body sticks out from the snow.

Save an empty advent calendar for **89**
next year. Swap your child's Advent
calendar with an empty one, along
with a note from the elf: "Time sure
does fly, doesn't it?"

Wrap the elf in toilet paper **90**
along with some figurines
and stuffed animals, all
saying: "Today is mummies
day."

91 Picture the elf getting ready to trim a doll's hair with scissors in hand.

92 Put the elf in a cup or mug of water with a straw. Include the note: "Blow into the straw to make my jacuzzi work".

The elf got stuck with his **93**
bottom poking out of a
cupboard. When we open it, we
find him munching on cakes
and leaving crumbs everywhere.

I tucked the elf under the sofa
cushions with his bottom **94**
sticking out. When we lifted the
cushions, we found children's
toys and objects that had been
missing for several days.

95 Unscrew a few light bulbs and place them in a tiny bag as if a mischievous elf had taken them during the night.

96 The elf is now sitting among DVD and music CD covers. Oh no, he mixed up all the CDs with the wrong jackets!

Secure a variety of figurines and lock them up in glass jars **97** or containers. Include a message from the elf saying, "Welcome to my zoo!"

Create binoculars using two toilet paper rolls and position **98** the elf by the window to spy on the neighbors. You can share a little about what he saw last night.

99 Hang shoes by their laces on the coat rack or door handles. Put the elf inside a shoe.

100 On the day the elf departs, get a small suitcase ready for him. Fill it with the items he took from the kids - toys, toothbrushes, stuffed animals... Let your imagination run wild!

Here's a sample of a letter that Elfie can write on the day it leaves:

Hey Family, I'm heading back to the North Pole soon. Just wanted to drop you a note to say thank you for the amazing time I had with you. Waking up in your cozy home every morning brought me so much happiness. Your smiles, laughter, and Christmas spirit made my days brighter.

I really enjoyed getting ready little surprises for you each day. It made me so happy to see your faces light up when you found my new pranks. I hope my adventures have brought you as much joy as they have brought me.

I want to thank you for being so kind, curious, and fun. You made my time here truly special. I'll keep you in my heart and treasure these memories until we see each other again next year.

Wishing you a Merry Christmas and a fantastic New Year! Remember to take care of yourself and keep spreading love and joy. I'll be keeping an eye on you from the North Pole, getting ready to come back next year with more surprises and happiness.

With lots of love and a touch of playfulness, Your Mischievous Elf

Don't forget to always keep smiling and laughing, it's the key to keeping the magic of Christmas alive all year long!

Made in United States
Troutdale, OR
12/18/2024

26806404R00037